I0547893

I WANDERED, LOST

poems

KRISTINA BROOKE DANIELE

Foreword by SELENA FLEMING
edited by TAMEKA ALLEN-COTTO
cover designed by JON STUBBINGTON

published by kristina brooke daniele

published by kristina brooke daniele

ISBN: 978-1-7362262-1-6 (ebook)

ISBN: 978-1-7362262-0-9 (physical)

❀ Created with Vellum

to my hurricane
my perfect storm
my safe space
my true north

inside

forward   vii

informed   1

woke   7

anthem   11

not for consumption   17

descend   21

enduring fallacy   27

reveal   35

exhilarate   39

destitute   43

languish   47

obeisance   51

seen   55

transform   61

about   65

forward

Kristina is my sister - the kind of sister the Universe stitches to you because it knows that kindred souls like yours need not tarry alone. It knows that you deserve to see your scars, humor, and beauty reflected back to you in ways that stoke the sun in your eyes.

She is the kind of sister you don't meet until the right words are written at the time to tether you in the right moment.

And when the moment arrived, we would learn that we lived and grew up in the same city, minutes from each other, probably traveling the same routes, and eating at the same places. We would learn that our experiences and childhoods were eerily familiar. But more important, we would learn that we shared a love for the spoken and written word. Words that cajole and bite and sing. Words that break us open for all the world to see and mend us back into a form of ourselves. For me, her words have always been that and more. So when she asked me to write the foreword, I gladly said yes.

"i wandered lost" is equal parts spiritual, magical, and ancestral. It is a journey, an intimate foretelling of raw vulnerability wrapped in delicate wonder and power. It is a summons to the masses to see its broken spaces and concede its duty to heal. It tenderly cross-weaves the echoes of yesterday's ghosts with the ashes of tomorrow's triumphs. Its words are beautiful, melodic, and transformative granting Black women the freedom to just *be*. It points north, showing us how to unfurl our secrets and bare our truths.

"i wandered lost" is wonderfully crafted poetic verse. I am marred by its words, better for having basked in its audacity and brilliance. Kristina's words have always stirred me, collapsing and expanding my understanding of grit and grace, and "i wandered lost" is no exception.

Kristina, I know this has been a long time coming. You did it sis and it is mah-velous!

- Selena Fleming, poet

informed

(to know)

i'm an expert at many things

like widened eyes
and crooked smiles
and silent conversations
like scolding tongues
and phrases of disapproval
lips pursed in opposition
and stiffening at your touch

i'm an expert at many things
like planning out my days
and not living them
i make promises that go unfulfilled
i hope without action
give without receiving

i'm an expert at so many things
too many to count
and yet i fail at being what i need
and loving myself

between sorrows and hiccuped sobs

between heartbeats and shivers
between robotic days and sleepless nights
i'm learning to be free

between nightmares and awkward silence
between loss and rediscovery
between sweat-filled panics and emptiness
i'm learning to be me

woke

(to awake from slumber)

before i understood, i knew

i knew the pain of racism
before phrases like *white supremacy* and *implicit bias* lodged
    their meaning into my lexicon
i knew
i knew my dark-skin and how it glistened in the sun was a sight
    to behold
there was no love for my tight coils
for my full lips
nor my thick thighs

gifted they labeled me
as if intelligence was an anomaly for us
their eyes widened in shock three black children shared the
    same parents
they looked with curiosity and fear
with longing and dread
i noticed

i noticed the descriptors
a *black neighborhood*
a *black author*

black music
they said *well-spoken* and *articulate*
but what they didn't say was louder

so you see i'm not woke
being black in america means you don't get to sleep
not even when you want to
you don't get to breathe or run or die with dignity
you get reminders of your place
to beg for your humanity
to pretend to be ok

because you're our ancestors' wildest dreams
you can't stop
you get exhaustion
but you don't get sleep…
or life

-for Breonna Taylor, whose murderers still have not been
   charged

anthem

(an uplifting verse that unites a group)

we were thrown together

to live where blood wasn't thicker than ego or shame, where
   truth was never the same twice and forgiveness could come
   only in death

we were dressed in easter's finest
hair designed by Kim & Steve

before they got caught up in drugs and disease

we learned to hate those who could do what we could not
we spit on those not privy to what we got

but freedom would come if we paid its price
4 slashes of sharpened tongue
5 welts of extensions cords or
being forced to sleep in the tub

in the end we learned nothing is given for free
not being born or adopted

this is my home

sea to shining sea flows with the blood and sweat of stolen lives
our eyes swollen with tears
fears grip me at night
urging me to take flight to return to where my body can be
where black is free

this is my home
in states stitched together by the never-ending rope used to
    lynch me
though reminders of hate stand and truth burns in bursts of lies
and false messiahs holster privilege to be used as
weapons of mass destruction like obstructions of justice woven
    together by corruption of might
our souls shine in foundations of white houses
say can you see old glory stained with amber waves of shame?

this is my home
every acre is owed
to ancestors with black faces
standing tall in spite of scarred backs

unbroken and healing

in the light of the rising sun let us march on 'til victory is won

not for consumption

(to remain unused as a resource)

i will not cut open my soul

will not bleed my every fear or make my pain your meme

i will not expose my rawness to disconnected ignorance or
superficial concern

i will not bleed my every fear

descend

(to fall lower)

sometimes i am too aware

of what is happening in my brain
i am too attuned to the chemical manifestation of despair
i sense the too-human-smell of myself
i feel each labored breath scrape against my skin with precision
pain draws a map my brain will not and cannot decipher
like jonathan livingston seagull i long to reach new heights
i keep trying
for love
while living
makes me ache
to walk off a cliff
to plummet to the bottom
to find peace in the sinking
to still time
for freedom

of all the sounds i've ever heard

death is the loudest

enduring fallacy

(a unsound belief continues to be believed)

'love' my mother said

when i was still young
enough to believe in fairy tales of happily ever after
'does not exist'
her voice red and stern
leaving no space for disagreement
no what ifs
her disappointment was solid
immovable
so i gave myself without love
to the pretense of love
to bodies that spoke of love in the counting
of deficits and expectations
and we faked it until we were appeased
in dark sweaty moments of physical sensations
of skin and musk and
fluids and want and
need and fuck me hard on rooftops of buildings
from which she warned me away

i entered deserted fields with strangers
and undeserved trust

looking and learning
love seeks and finds the darkest of souls
yet it is neither doe-eyed nor
rosy cheeked

love begins a seedling
rooting during pregnant diatribes
when a mother pleads with you to walk away from her son
because you deserve more than a house of children you
    can't feed

love is the absent father gone six years who
returns as you abort all signs of rebellion
compassionate eyes reminding you that you are not alone

love comes and goes in downward spirals of darkness--
loneliness and disappointment aloneness
in manic cycles of frenzied self-harm
through acid-induced trysts with barely-known boys
who like girls simply to be liked by boys
and girls who spend days not liking themselves
while guzzling putrid
mad dog 20/20
and weed
and games of seduction
and dangerous lies

'love lives' he whispers in the darkness as one foot hangs over
    the edge of swirling madness
and sadness
and fear

so you try to believe
that love lives in the ridiculous idea
to cross a football field in a blizzard for cigarettes
and as the labored breaths turn into asthmatic gasps for air

you sink into each other's arms
knowing something feels right

love peers through tear-filled eyes in hospital rooms
love stains your cheeks
as you deliver your baby too fragile to survive in a world where
    love is a myth

'love does not exist' she reminds before abandoning us to a loss
    she warns will destroy
yet we hold each other
we shield each other
through another high-risk pregnancy
and death
and debt
and estrangement

we learn
and grow
and relearn
and remember

love doesn't just exist
love is created
through pain
and excitement
and fear
and in quiet moments of shared understanding
it breaks through the cracks
to grow in concrete

i thought i'd be dead by now

thought i'd give up or give in
or somehow my heart would give out
because life ends when lessons are learned
or when the only thing left is silence

reveal
_____

(to show what's hidden)

in the morning light you'll see my scars

and you'll know my secret
i am only human
magical yet real
and buried
under plans
failed
forgotten
hopes lost
and dreams rotten left alone
deferred until the morning

you'll see my scars
and you'll run

exhilarate

(bringing or evoking energy)

he does to me what i never expected

he leaves me open
heart bleeding
untethered and clinging
to a hardness that i toss
like a weapon of emotional destruction

yet i shed fears
instead of tears
break down walls
and unlock doors to let him in
and it's not something i was taught
i saw nothing of love at the hands she balled into fists
ready to punctuate me with exclamations

inadequate
undesirable
unworthy of love

what i learned was to lie
to falsify my thoughts
never really hoping that the outcome

would prove me better
better than her warnings
better than those who forgot me and left me to die
in her cold arms
leaving me to long for a mother
only to replace her
with lover
after lover
when one could not be found

i wandered lost

the strength of arms gripping me
pulling me from
securing me in
hope renewed
he does to me what a syncopated beat does
to a repeated melody played without originality
until regret is the loudest whisper and death a relief
he makes me live

destitute

(lacking subsistence)

maybe as you stood breathing in the fire

of your inadequacies
packed tightly into a blunt of despair
you thought i was worth the journey

maybe you knew
for love to escape it has to burst
through bated breaths and
tear apart illusions

maybe you knew the price was too high
or maybe i knew
and that's why i walked away

languish

(undergo neglect)

love is a painful journey

tumultuous
love consumes
it burns
love reduces
it depletes
love leaves us
in ruins
and build us up

obeisance

(a movement that expresses deep respect like a bow)

for octavia chloe yolanda and marguerite

i am muse
child of divination
born on the congo
an artist
a force
an error so correct i never need to be checked
i foretell evil's demise
i am beloved
bursts of light searing the sahara
nourishing the ancestors you've tried to kill
i am reverence
you cannot replace me you will not erase me
i rise

seen
—————

(to be observed with depth)

i wanted to grow

(up)
big strong protected
(on pedestals)
so i lied
(created for evasion)
escaped hurt and inflicted pain
(not pride)
i wanted to be free
(in spite of you)
despite you
(instead i came)
to spite you
(to despise you)
but i could not escape you
(until i faced the truth)
with my truth
(love and fear cannot coexist)
and eventually i will
(and with time I will)
forget you (forget you)

i want just one moment

of being picture perfect
surrounded by love

to know how it would feel
to have her wipe away my tears
i want just one moment

hearing her cheer from the bleachers
pride on her face as i take the shot
of being picture perfect

how would it feel to know that i am enough
and surrounded by love

transform

(to change in structure

they wanted to devour

to **stifle** me
to keep me bound to **doubt**
instead i **emerge** from the ruins of them **to become**
unwavering a force with unshakeable resolve
sprouting **wings of** self-assurance
i became more than the sum of my broken heart

she wanted to extinguish my **light** to warp and taint
my soul
to kill me
instead i **burn** her with the holiness of me
i expel the disease of doubt
i find the cure
with my fragmented reflection of **the smallest shimmer**
of hope
in the strength of **me**

about the book

it's hard to explain this book as i believe each poem speaks for itself
although its meaning changes with the various experiences brought to
its reading

while this book is reflective of the various parts of who i am and what
I've felt it is also a letter to the universe

i am learning and growing

about the author

kristina brooke daniele is learning to be less critical of herself as she works to become the author she has always wanted to become currently kristina lives in arizona but is originally from the bronx in new york kristina enjoys reading website design mixed media art and writing homeschooling lessons for her child her husband andrew is her greatest fan and he is often close by encouraging her in her many ventures including homeschooling their child and protecting them both from the people

when not writing or reading kristina can be found hanging out with her family singing karaoke watching the family dog sir issac gutenberg aggressively sniff and search for the food he's already eaten but thinks his humans have hidden often she indulges in the possibilities of unscripted looking-for-love shows and romance movies

acknowledgements

andrew: you continue to be my support to lift me up when i fall
and to remind me who i really am when i sometimes forget
thanks for walking this planet with me i love you

mya: thanks for making me see the world with fresh eyes you
challenge me to be who i say i am and to lead by example; i
am encouraged by your bravery because of that life is
brighter i love you

caroline kennedy-wilson: our lives are an ongoing book of
emotions and life lessons and through it all we find
ourselves closer; i am honored to call you sister and friend.

selena fleming: i don't know where to begin and i can't
remember the moment i realized that soul-sisters are real
but i know that my spirt has been drawn to yours since we
met thanks for your inspiration, love, clarity, and words i
am honored to call you friend

tameka allen-cotto: your edits have made my words shine
thanks for your support and your friendship and of course

the shoulder tears and laughs! i love you! me and you of hue 'til the end

catherine atkinson and machelle cox: encouraging me to read my poem at the open mic made me remember how much i love writing woo juice extra woo on me

kevin johnson (coach kj): i don't like kevins but i like you! thanks for making me look deeper for reminding me that i don't need acceptance; just respect and thank you for challenging me even when i pushed back you are an amazing human!

brooke lay: your friendship means so much to me and i'm am happy that age has made us wiser i love you! thanks for the reads the photos of the little man and the memories

my writing sisters: shadae trotman donyae dillman kenya goree-bell and **moni boyce** your insights suggestions countless reads and friendship has given me so much courage thanks for your magic!

niesha sweet: so yeah i finally did it; you pushed me to extend my boundaries and managed to cure my claustrophobia :) thank you for your support and friendship

also by kristina brooke daniele

Civil Rights Then & Now: a Timeline History of the Fight for Equality in America by Kristina Brooke Daniele